To David and Catherine
In appreciation of our
shared love of Art
in all its forms!

30.3.2021

Inside – Outside

A Collection of Poems

Linda Line

xx

GH00808306

By Linda Line

Photo & Graphic Credits

All photos by Linda Lines except:
Old black & white family photos.
Logo: A collaboration between Oscar Lines
and Hagar@littlegreenmonkey.co.uk
Graphics: Little Green Monkey Limited.

Cover image taken at:
Gallerie Va Bene
1, place Bouet
La Romieu
32480

About Linda

My life has been a series of reinventions:

I was raised in the West Country, but my father's and first husband's RAF postings gave me an appetite for travel. My favourite subject in a somewhat disrupted education was child psychology. This led to my setting up a nursery school in Singapore after my son was born, which I ran for a wonderful 10 years — and then applied to working with businessmen.

And so, to London:

My next 22 years were in the City where I founded The Lines Partnership, a small financial management company which prospered until I sold out, free to pursue the four passions which now inspire me: writing poetry, photography, cooking and travel. All happily combined in my first book Men In My Kitchen.

Whilst writing poetry seems more important to me than anything else now, I would say the inspiration comes from my photography. The photos come first and, as often as not, I see life through the ever-improving lens of a smartphone.

This has led to a desire to understand the technology behind communication in today's world, and the extraordinary new language that goes with it — how to produce e-books, the importance of a website with a blog, and the mixed blessings of social media.

I'm happy to say I am, after this second book, more comfortable in all these areas, and getting better each day.

———

Website & blog: www.lindalines.co.uk

———

Facebook: facebook.com/lindajlines
Twitter: @lindajlines
Instagram: Windowsofthewrld

Introduction

"Inside – Outside" is a very different, small collection of poems and images.

It is all of me… It is today… It is my truth.

Little heartfelt pieces and reflections of here and now, which I should like to share.

It is a celebration of having made it thus far,

And discovering life can just get better…

In spite of worldwide turmoil and division, and areas of great pain and suffering,

The hardest of obstacles can be overcome with the right frame of mind.

A big slice of optimism, imagination, a hell of a lot of hard work and determination helps…

If you are lucky enough to be in a safe and secure enough place to indulge it.

Thankfully — for the moment — I am.

Most of all, I believe in as much kindness as you can find in your heart to give.

Kindness is my favourite word.

Quotes

"Only remember the good things
— forget the rest."

FROM MY GRANDMOTHER

Mind is the Master power that moulds and makes,
And Man is Mind, and evermore he takes
The tool of Thought, and, shaping what he wills,
Brings forth a thousand joys, a thousand ills:
He thinks in secret, and it comes to pass:
Environment is but his looking-glass.

FROM JAMES ALLEN 1864 - 1912

Imagination is the supreme faculty of the mind.
Imagine a thing continually
And it will be realised.

FROM KAHLIL GIBRAN'S *THE PROPHET*
who clearly agrees with James Allen

Words of wisdom that have kept me on track all
through my life.

I hope my new book is as uplifting for you as it has
been for me in its making.

Contents

Inside

Outside

Taste of Thailand

Inside

A Tribute

My mother's kitchen when I was young
Thinking of it – I am undone –
Where the shaping of me began
My love of cooking even then
Certainly no sign of men,
Away at War.
Just my big sister, little brothers and me
Life felt so free…
The Second World War had come and gone
Leaving hardship of which we knew none
Too young.
I remember rationing – the norm
To learn to do without – we did.
Hard work in the kitchen – no choice.
I hear my mother's voice.
A little imagination goes a long way
Make something taste good
With no eggs, butter and sugar
If you could
Such scarcity,
Luxury food a rarity…
Steamed puddings and dumplings in stew,

She really knew how to do.
We learned – fast
Things that would last…
A lifetime.
We survived
But never said thank you before she died

Ageless Youth

I let my face fall back into place...
As much as it can.
I want this day…
The pace quickens

How to beat time?
I'm frightened, I'm awed
I will squeeze life
And give thanks
This urgency, this knowledge

Time to get up
The heart races
Bend, stretch – breathe
Treat me well it pleads
So, I do
With loving care…

Dishwasher

Lonely wineglass in the dishwasher
Hits home
It takes a long time to fill and shouts
"Alone"
In that mathematical sense I am,
But I like it a lot… And
I am free to choose when not.

Lonely?
Definitely not.
It's a choice and taken a lifetime
To give it voice.
I've had my fill of pretenders
Of deceivers
And greedy non-believers.

I've set myself free
And found time
To believe in me.
Tomorrow there will be a second glass.
In the slow-to-fill dishwasher.
… It's mine, not his.
Pass the bottle.

Just Before Dawn

Thoughts and words rise to the top like cream:
Try to catch them uncluttered
Before they melt away like a dream
In those waking moments before dawn.
They have filtered in uninvited and unworn
To be recorded and set free
To light up what's deep inside of me.
Then sounds intrude that seek to end

That purity of thought might bend
As guilt and anxiety filter in…
Hurry now, the rush begins —
Then voices of a different kind
Clutter up the mind.
They are not content
Until all beauty is snuffed out
Please… don't shout!

This small battle has been won
To say what's been said
Before guilt pushes me out of bed,
Before outside comes in

And claims ownership and wins,
But there's another
Habit which takes control…
The hand is forced to switch it on.

The air waves have won
And smother all the natural thoughts
That flow inside our heads
To influence what was ours
And bow us to their will: when to think and feel…
Everything we are and own, they steal.
This android world has hold of us
and forces us to act…

A very frightening fact…
It's coming from all sides now:
How easy to succumb.
Original thinking numbed
Those mobile electronic sounds that summon us
Just like a baby's urgent cry
We have to reach and pick it up
To discover what comes next

The World Wide Web dictates…
'Ping'… we have to text…

Middle of the Night

Lost
The first line
Escapes
Half asleep
Powerful
To the point
And mine
Unique, delicate and fine
A phrase

Evaporated like steam
As in a dream
No longer there
It told the truth
Like no other
Pitch perfect
Just out of reach
I feel it still
Come back I beseech
That sound
Just underground.

Acceptance

Milestones
…Acceptance
…Inevitability.
Tell-tale signs
Hands, arms
Face first, neck
Scaly shins
No matter how often
You exfoliate
Lavish with oil, creams
It's too late…
Elasticity has given in
High necks and tight-fitting jeans
That hug you in
Wear quality Lycra in the gym
Keep slim
And active
Don't let age in…
Without a fight
Do it!…
You can!
So I did.

Memory

Memories start to dim
Especially short term
The old chestnuts remain loyal
Names and words
Amnesia creeps in...
"Now, where was I?"
Standing looking in
The fridge…
Can't remember why.
A place for everything
A must,
And everything in its place
Unless it's not!
Who moved that?
New ideas, reinvent yourself
Stimulate, don't capitulate.
What did you always want to do
And never did?
Do it!
You can.
So, I did.

Passion is Ageless

Grow old… gracefully they say
Or disgracefully for some
Don't forget dignity…
Oh pray!
Sounds so sedentary
What of passion?
You frown, as if it is something
To be outgrown
Reserved for the young alone
Who may feel distaste at what
Remains in my head, in my heart
And in my far from dead body…
The process of ageing is just that
A process…
A collection of experiences of touch and taste
Of hardship and happiness
Of excess… of waste.
But in youth – I remember there is no haste
Life stretches endlessly ahead
An eternity… You think
In an instant gone.
But not so the passion
For life, for love…
Love?...
It's ageless.

Sisters

It comes back to bite
In spite of old age.
You'd think I'd be over that stage
By now,
But it's back to haunt me again.
When I have so much
I want to share.
Why are the old feelings still there?
When my sister comes to stay?

She assumes that big sister stance
And I'm diminished in one glance
By a well-placed word
Judgmental, critical,
Often disagreeable
And then damned with faint praise
...The worst!
It's really absurd.
Now in our seventies
With grandchildren too
We still jostle for position
And never listen...

Or say we're proud
Of each other out loud
And we are.
But if she's hurt or sick
Or another criticises...
Sisters,
An impregnable force.
No one more protective.
Whatever happens
We're still there for each other.
I guess it's just what sisters do.

Looking Back

Was it my insecurity
… Or envy?
Was it always thus,
Because I was taller
And she smaller
And darker?
Perhaps it was why
My golden curls
Got pulled.

I had envy too…
She was older
And bolder.
"Can I come with you?"
I'd say.
"It's time you were in bed"
…I followed, and she led.
I wished I'd been a boy…
So, did my father.
Two girls could not bring him the joy
He craved.
So he didn't notice me much,
The early affection saved…

For his firstborn
And then the brothers who followed
I was lost in the middle.

But nature was kind to me.
So, said my mother,
Who could plainly see
My pain.
She set me free.
I loved her most for that.
It gave me drive and a determination.
Proud now to be seen…
A show-off I'd been.
It gave me the confidence too
To do what I've done
And say what I do…
To be me.
Albeit at times
Defiantly,
Defensively.
We are products of our childhood.
We bury the sad, and bad,
And remember the funny and good
We learn… and now pretty much are understood.
Thus it ever was – I'm glad…
To have a beloved big sister.

True and Straight and Tall

It's harder being a woman than a man
No one told me so when small.
Only work as hard as you can
Stand true and straight and tall …
So I did.
Then four brothers came along…
Mum said the same to them
And taught us all as one.
It paid off in many ways
And set the bar high.
We could reach for the sky, she said.
So we did.
My brothers treat women the same as men
And I do too… But
A very different journey I have had.
The way was hard for me in
A world of kids not brought up
Like us.

There have been men I've loved
And lost along the way
Who couldn't handle that I could think,

Challenge and say –
In exactly the same way.
A novelty, even attractive at first,
And then rage –
That I stood firmly on the same page.

Not content until they'd broken
Or diminished to put me in my place.
We both lost face – and departed.
No winners in that race.
So, mothers, will you,
Tell your sons and daughters all
Stand true, and straight and tall?

Millennials

A halo around the sound…
Of voices
Listing choices
Coming from all directions
At them
I close my eyes and focus,
Listen, share the pain
Threading my attention
through the eye of a needle…
where is their direction
Now?
Tried and applied,
Learned and loved.
On screen.
It's fiction
Passion is illusory
Lonely
Fashion as fickle
Magazine cover

All over them
They love…
They love me not.

More Voices
More choices
Looking…
Away from satanical
Temptations
Let's hide, it's mechanical
It's macho
New passion
Yesteryear bikes
The resonance
The speed
It's fanatical
The romance
Run away
Where?
Escape not the solution
The knowledge the need
To accumulate
Education
Brings power… It's
How to succeed
That's the promise.
So…
How to stop the noise?

What Makes a Poet?

Rough edges polished to a shine
By pain past
Same as mine
Life reflected through a prism
That exaggerated light
Touch, taste and sight
Through knowing eyes –
Not recognised.
I see it as a gift, not
An oddity to dismiss –
Oft ridiculed by those less blessed. –
Cruelty and kindness, we've seen it all.

The see-saw of extremes
That pulled and pushed us
In and out of dreams.
In maturity a calm is reached
As words come into play
That float above the debris
And allow us now our say.
Words lift and lighten and brighten

In quite a different way…
I write them down…
And keep them.

Honesty

I thought I had scared you off with my honesty
My talk of La La Land
I do that when I'm moved
You unsettled me.
I told you so, I wish I hadn't
Too much too soon?

I shy away from strong
You were bold
Was it a defence –
Or all about control?
I'm too old for that.
Nothing made any sense
Such talents we two,
Too much too soon.

Too practised to be out of depth.
Easier to get out of the way
Bury emotions the moment
They have something to say.
It's easier that way.
Honestly?
I'm not asking for the moon
Too much too soon?

Chemistry

Chemistry discovered
Not enough
The moment ruled
Balance lost
No control
Freedom threatened
Peace of mind
Disintegrated
Not the me I like to be
In his thrall… momentarily
Needy
Caught in his long-legged headlights
Exciting, frightening
Depleted
Runaway!

Trust

Trust takes time
It's me that's the achiever
Don't apologise,
Don't be demeaned
By a charming receiver
of my generosity
with an agenda.
Why feel guilty?
He is not my problem.
Perhaps I would like him to be… And I'll not
run away
This time…

Sour Grapes and Sweet Sweet Lies

Dismissing sour grapes
With deadly nightshade
Feeling like a gooseberry fool
Dropping Baked Alaska
The pretence
Warm on the outside
Ice cold within —
As much a sin
As devils
On horseback
Wrapped in
Smokey
Streaky
Bacon
A sweet disguise
Plums transformed
Into wrinkled prunes
Truth will out those
Sweet sweet lies.

My Things

Nothing obvious
No gems, no jewels
Paintings? Maybe some
It's the oddities
With history
Emotions attached
Along life's journey
Hair toggles and clips
Luxuries – a well worn
Slinky slip
When I was thin.
Silk pyjamas
On my skin
A jewellery box
An Aladdin's cave
Of memories.

Red

Lipstick on
It's red, it's rich
Gets me out of bed
It transforms
It distracts
From unpalatable facts
Hides wrinkles and flaws
It diverts
It lifts
And lasts all day…

Outside

Vying for Attention

Attention seeking, they just muscle in...
They can't help themselves
Fighting for the limelight.
Give them an inch... They'll take a mile
But only for a while.

I snap the resilient geraniums
On fire and engine red...
Then have to smile...
Whilst they take their long life in their stride
They have their pride
And pragmatically step aside.

I glimpse a brilliance hard-won
Smiling back at me,
Stealing their window of opportunity,
And forgive...
Their short-term bravery so hard won
Against an unremitting sun...

Slip Sliding

Slip sliding
Riding
Rowing, cheeks glowing
River flowing
out
Glistening gleaming
Sticky -
reeling in
My emotions

All of Me

Sitting under my cherry tree,
Little pieces of me coloured green.
Tastes and smells of pink blossom
If you look there is all of me.
Water falling quietly, rhythmically
Into a pond full of life
Mirroring spaces and faraway places loved.
An Asian Buddha in this mix
Mindfully inside of me.
A journey to a better self.

Coming of Age

A lone Rose in this sea of green
Makes a play for centre stage
It's nearly come of age
And simply wants to show off,
Just this once… Before the crowd
A host of others way too proud
Who want to muscle in.
"Move over, your stem's much too thin"
Don't budge, hold your ground
Don't let those bullies in…
Use those sharp young thorns
Just shine
You still can win…

July Celebration – I

With sunflowers he came to me
A July celebration
Of my birthday, and their creation.
These noble champions of flowers
At their glorious best they have to be…
Just see the way they look at me
Directly with open faces
More yellow than the sun was
On that day the world began
It's tender promise to nourish…
Life in all its complexity, to flourish…

Nothing makes my heart soar
Nothing moves me more
Than the acres of golden symmetry
That stretch before my eyes
In July…
No soldiers manage such neat geometry
Radiant… So disciplined and brave
Standing still and tall
I feel so small…

Against that merciless gaze
Of the burning sun they try to imitate
To stare it out… and won't be fazed.
Sunflowers are more than brave.
I will them to out-dazzle
And hold their heads up higher
So valiantly, so joyfully
More defiantly… so suicidally…

But how long can it last?
This majesty…?
Only until July is past.
A travesty?
Oh no, they evolve thus,
Without fuss.

August– II

Arrives with searing heat –
Heads heavy now… They can't compete
Their job is nearly done, but
Sunflowers admit no defeat

The weight of seeds pregnant with oil
In burnt brown uniforms…
These heroes won't let the elements spoil
What they have valiantly won –
A rich harvest yet to come
They protect what weighs them down
And dip their heads and fiercely frown

Birds, better away, away!
These guardian soldiers here to stay
Until the farmer has his say,
One bright early September day…
Those noble toppled blooms reply,
Shed no tear, we will be back…
Next July…
And so shall I.

Summer Sandals

Overnight Spring exploded
Into bright colours
Spirits reloaded and soared
In an instant, awakened my soul.
This harsh winter long
Sub-zero to heatwave
In a song...
Winter clothes begone,
Summer sandals... on.

Sunflowers Sleep Too

The day was long for them.
Many more to go before July is out
But oh… the triumph felt
At each day's end.
When the sun shows weakness too
As it dips its head in shared relief
No longer trying to compete,
They hold on to belief
This blessed respite…

A laziness invades as
The bees are polite
And hum their soporific tune.
No, there's no more fight
They nod their heads in rows of unison
To the new moon
Whose gentle smile will be their mantle
Until day breaks… All too soon.

Thames Towpath Days

A quiet moment in time
I walk, I see
Architecture, poetry and romance
At every glance
A reflective millpond filled to the brim
That pauses to think
Draws breath
Capturing the last light
Of day
Before it is sucked away.

I bike, I pedal – a new day
The wind is strong, the water whipped
Tidal debris in my way
I have tripped
And waded ankle-deep
On paths —
Tides so high
They spilled over my feet

Seasons

Winter coat of subdued colours
Early morning gloom beckons
Misty breath competes
In seconds
Branches naked and cold.
The sun a token nod at noon
Lending reflections that deepen to orange
The afternoon slides past
Swiftly into night – too soon
I blink.
Spring has nudged in
With a speed and energy
Like no other season
A kaleidoscope

You lose your reason
Those vibrant colours
Win warmth and position
Along the river bank
A carpet to please and tease
Blossoms and buds
Bow out in the strong March breeze.
To April
With many a guise
Dress in layers if you're wise
Showers offer no surprise
Fooled by summer heat
May will just compete
A summer fraud with a promise
To stay
Reluctantly takes a back seat

To stronger
June, July and August
Who steal time...
Nonchalantly
and linger
Endlessly...

September filters in
With a mixed grin
Pretending to be what it is not
Disguised as summer
But we are under
No illusions – so wise
Full of surprise
Mimicking all
As it heads reluctantly towards glorious fall

I button up

October takes the prize
Banishing the summer haze
Crisp and bright
Heavy in reds and golds
All shades – falling
Richly at our feet
Their stories told
Burying them knee deep
A warm blanket
In waiting
For tides and winter snows.

Sunflowers S-t-r-e-t-ch

I strive,

I stretch...

Outstrip,

Reach...

For the stars
Breaking out of those
Well behaved rows
And sometimes I trip
I pause,
and grow another arm
To outstrip.

I will not be outdone
Will not hesitate —
Such a short life —
To make my mark
And eclipse

I will not conform

To the norm
I'll kick up a storm first.
I did…
I made my point
With head held higher
I look.
I see what they cannot.
New horizons.
S-t-r-e-t-ch….

Taste of Thailand

Hua Hin Days

Joy of joys
Another day begins
In faraway Hua Hin.
A turmoil of choices.
All senses invade,
Seductively pervade
All of me...
What is it about this place
That lifts me so?
The scarlet sun at the beginning
And end of each day?
It's reliable
Always there...
To warm my bones.
Beaches are silk between the toes
High tides are warmed milk.
The insistent urgent tones
Of another world's bird song.
I listen... spellbound.

Looking up I see
Colour to hurt my eyes.
Bougainvillea, a crimson flame
Spreading like fire,
Impossible to tame.
Close by,
Frangipani trees
Their fragrant white blossom
Floats down in the breeze
To my feet.
A host to orchids
In vibrant shades.
No parasite to me,
Their delicacy
Dependant on these
Architecturally beautiful trees.
A symbiotic relationship
If ever you please.

Intricately sliced pineapple,
Transformed in a trice
By a craftsman,
Who carves handles
To hold each slice,
That is so nice!
Papaya flesh so pink
Is that caviar inside?
Sorry no, but
Don't blink
At the ridiculous price.

Golden mangos,
Paired with rice,
That's sticky and sweet,
My favourite treat.
Bananas large and small
An incredulous, pendulous
flower comes first
Dwarfed by leaves so tall.
This fruit, cooked
Or not…
In batter
Any way at all,
It doesn't matter.

To quench your thirst
Freshly cut coconuts,
Flesh frozen in ice-cream
A dream…
There's more,
Passion-fruit, custard fruit
Green limes galore.
A kaleidoscope of colours
And tropical tastes
And smells,
I just want more.
Compulsively edible,
All incredible!

A land of noisy contrasts,
The voices, the endless music
A cacophony of sound
Of high notes and low
Of motorbikes and carts
Pushed so slow
Hair-raising traffic flow.
Stalls laden with food that is fast
And to eat on the go
With your fingers,
Or linger…

Fresh from the sea
Or the well farmed land
That is lush, where everything grows
Life ebbs and flows.
Combined with herbs and spices,
Nothing is bland
I just laugh out loud...
Ain't this grand?

Religion not intrusive
At all,
Just a way of life
That looks inside itself
Looking for self-improvement
Not strife…
And is not afraid to confront
Idolising body and soul
Showing respect for the old
And for those who achieve.
We like to please…
A better life, no envy.
It's Buddhism,
What's not to believe?
Make merit, be humble
Don't grumble…
Down on your knees!

Save the best to last
Indelibly scored:
The two-hour massage
Of course,
Coming my way
From ladies who smile
And are never bored.
Endless tranquillity,
Oil applied deftly,
So peacefully
And quietly
Time stands still.
I've taken the Hua Hin
Happiness pill...

Lightning Source UK Ltd.
Milton Keynes UK
UKHW022318200120
357287UK00002B/3